LOST CITY OF POMPEII

LOST CITY OF POMPEII

by

Dorothy Hinshaw Patent

BENCHMARK BOOKS

MARSHALL CAVENDISH
NEW YORK

Acknowledgments

With special thanks to J. Donald Hughes,
John Evans Professor
in the Department of History, University of Denver,
for his invaluable assistance in
reading the manuscript.

Benchmark Books
Marshall Cavendish Corporation
99 White Plains Road
Tarrytown, New York 10591-9001

Copyright © 2000 by Dorothy Hinshaw Patent

Library of Congress Cataloging-in-Publication Data
Patent, Dorothy Hinshaw.
Lost city of Pompeii / Dorothy Hinshaw Patent.
p.   cm. — (Frozen in time)
Includes bibliographical references and index.
Summary: Describes the destruction of Pompeii by the eruption of Mount Vesuvius
in 79 A.D. and how its rediscovery nearly 1700 years later provided information about
life in the Roman Empire.
ISBN 0-7614-0785-5
1. Pompeii (Extinct city)—Juvenile literature. [1. Pompeii (Extinct city) 2. Vesuvius
(Italy)—Eruption, 79.] I. Title. II. Series: Patent, Dorothy Hinshaw. Frozen in time.
DG70.P7 P38   1999   937'.7—dc21   99-34980   CIP   AC

Printed in Hong Kong

1 3 5 6 4 2

Photo research by Linda Sykes Picture Research, Hilton Head, SC
Book design by Carol Matsuyama

Photo Credits
Cover: e. t. archive; pages 18–19, 26–27: e. t. archive; page 54: Archaeological
Museum, Naples/e. t. archive; pages 2–3: Peter Bianchi/National Geographic Image
Collection, pages 38–39: Richard Nowitz/National Geographic Image Collection; pages 7,
14–15, 17, 21, 35, 40–41, 45, 53: David Hiser/Photographers Aspen; pages 8–9: Musée
Condé, Chantilly, France/Giraudon/Art Resource; page 30: Erich Lessing/Art Resource;
page 39: Museo Archaeologico Nazionale, Naples/Erich Lessing/Art Resource; pages 50–51:
Alinari/Art Resource; pages 11, 48: Superstock; pages 24–25, 47: Richard Nowitz; page 29:
Mimmo-Jodice/Corbis; pages 31, 43: Robert Harding; pages 32–33: Museo Archeologico
Nazionale, Naples/Roger-Viollet/Bridgeman Art Library; page 36: Accademia Italiana,
London/Bridgeman Art Library

Contents

Introduction

I once lived in the city of Naples, Italy. From our balcony, my husband and I could look across the Bay of Naples and see peaceful Mount Vesuvius. Every week a farmer who lived on the mountain brought chickens and eggs to our home. They were the best I ever ate. It's hard to believe that this beautiful mountain, its slopes covered by vineyards and farms, could ever have exploded and completely destroyed all life in nearby towns and farms.

While we lived in Naples, my husband and I visited the ruins of Pompeii, a Roman town buried beneath a deluge of rock and ash by an eruption of Mount Vesuvius in A.D. 79. Even though I saw Pompeii more than twenty-five years ago, I remember it clearly. As I walked the streets of this ancient ghost town, I felt time slip away. Almost two thousand years earlier, Roman people had walked these same streets and lived in these houses. Beautiful paintings decorated the walls of many homes where families had sat down to share meals. Ruts from carriage wheels in the main street spoke of the city's daily activity. I saw the forms of the bodies of some of the unlucky people who had been trapped by the eruption. Their impressions had been cast in plaster by archaeologists so that their last moments of suffering had been captured forever.

The similarities of life then and now especially impressed me. Mosaic decorations on the floors included one at the entrance to a house, showing a vicious-looking chained dog. Cave canem—*"beware of the dog"—was written beneath it. And just as we put signs on our lawns in support of candidates for office, so the people of Pompeii painted political slogans on the sides of their houses:* ALL THE FRUIT SELLERS WITH HELVIUS VESTALIS SUPPORT THE ELECTION OF M. HOLCONIUS PRISCUS AS DUUMVIR *(a political office). Back then, like today, people couldn't resist writing on the walls just because they were there, with statements such as "Everybody writes on the walls but me."*

Ever since my visit to Pompeii, I have been interested in what this

This mosaic of a dog at the entrance to a home in Pompeii was accompanied by the words Cave Canem, *"Beware of the Dog."*

city, truly frozen in time, can tell us about the way people lived from day to day during the height of the Roman Empire. Archaeologists have been learning from Pompeii for more than a hundred years. Even so, every year new discoveries add to our knowledge and understanding of society in those long-ago times.

1

DISASTER

August 24, A.D. 79, began like any other day for the inhabitants of Pompeii. The sun shone in a bright blue sky, markets were bustling, and people were going about their ordinary lives.

Then, around lunchtime, they heard a tremendous boom. The earth shook under their feet. Nearby Mount Vesuvius had blown its top, spewing millions of tons of rock and ash into a gigantic black cloud that towered above the landscape. The wind was blowing directly toward Pompeii from the volcano. Within moments ash and pumice (a light-weight volcanic rock full of tiny bubbles) began falling from the sky onto the city.

◄ *When Mount Vesuvius erupted in A.D. 79, no one expected it. It had not erupted for nearly 1,000 years. The mountain was to explode again. This painting shows Vesuvius erupting 1,700 years after it destroyed Pompeii.*

Many people panicked. They grabbed a few possessions and fled from town. Some ran to the harbor, hoping to escape by boat. Others stayed put.

Pumice and ash continued to fall, with inches of material dropping down every hour, until the ground was covered by several feet of rock

Anatomy of a Volcano

Vesuvius was a peaceful mountain for nearly a thousand years before that fateful day in A.D. 79. What made Vesuvius burst forth so violently and cause such vast destruction?

The source of volcanic activity lies deep beneath the surface of the earth. Underneath the earth's thick top layer of solid rock, called the crust, lies the mantle, a region of liquid rock. Below the mantle, at the center of the earth, is the core. The core is thought to be made of nickel and iron. The outer part of the core is hot liquid. The difference in temperature between the earth's hot core and its cool crust sets up currents in the liquid rock that lies between them.

The crust isn't an unbroken layer of rock. It is made up of many pieces, like a jigsaw puzzle. These pieces, which actually float on top of the mantle, are called tectonic plates. In some places where two plates meet, the currents in the mantle cause one plate to be pushed under the other. The friction between them creates heat, which is believed to melt the rock of the plate that is being pushed under. This melted rock is called magma.

Volcanoes are mounds, hills, or moun tains formed when magma flows to the surface of the earth. The magma contains gases, which create pressure that builds up underground. The gases eventually push the liquid rock up to the surface through cracks in the crust. Magma that flows to the surface is called lava. When the lava meets the air, it slowly cools and hardens. Little by little, the volcano grows. Ash and pieces of rock also build the volcano. A volcano that grows in this way usually does little or no harm to human life, although it can destroy property.

Some volcanoes erupt violently, however. If hardened lava has closed a volcano's vents, or openings, the magma has no way to escape and its gases continue to build up. Eventually, something has to give. Many scientists think that an earthquake that occurred in Pompeii in A.D. 62 helped create the Vesuvius eruption. They think that the earthquake was caused by the shifting of tectonic plates beneath Vesuvius. The shifting caused more magma to form beneath Vesuvius. The magma and its gases collected inside the volcano, and pressure on the volcano's hard lava plug increased. In A.D. 79, the plug finally burst, and ash, rock, and gases hurtled into the atmosphere and ash. The city was in total darkness. The people who remained tied pillows or roof tiles onto their heads to protect themselves from the continuous bombardment. They had no idea what sort of disaster had befallen them and thought their homes were the safest place to be.

Unfortunately, they were wrong. After about twelve hours, the

During a volcanic eruption, streams of lava and deadly gases flow down the mountainside.

force of the eruption slowed down so that the pumice and ash fell upon the slopes of the volcano instead of rocketing into the sky. This volcanic debris, mixed with deadly gases, then sped down the mountain in glowing avalanches.

Up until this time, the town of Herculaneum, which lay on the shore of the Bay of Naples to the northwest of Pompeii, had only experienced a little ashfall. Many residents had gathered along the shore, probably hoping to escape in boats. But Herculaneum lay right in the path of the surge of volcanic material racing down the slopes of Vesuvius. The flow hit the town with such force that it blew down walls and tossed the rubble several feet. The people awaiting rescue had gathered in storage chambers where boats were kept, but there was no escape. All were killed, some by the heat of the avalanche, others by choking on the ash-laden air.

At about seven-thirty on the morning of August 25, an avalanche hit what was left of Pompeii. The two thousand or so people who had survived up to this time, stumbling around in the dark on top of almost eight feet (2.4 meters) of pumice and ash, all died.

After the eruption, the sky remained dark for two or three days. When it cleared, survivors could see that the entire top of Vesuvius was gone. A broad crater about two miles (3.2 kilometers) wide was left. All that could be seen of Pompeii were the tops of some buildings rising above the volcanic fallout. Herculaneum had been buried by a flow of hot gases, ash, and rock so deep that nothing remained in sight.

The eruption of Vesuvius devastated the entire Bay of Naples area. Ash and rock fell as far as forty-six miles (seventy-four kilometers) away, and at least 3,600 people died.

Few people ever returned to Pompeii. Some looters dug beneath the ash and found objects of value. Others found pockets of poisonous gas. As time went by and generations passed, memory of the event gradually faded. By the time the Roman Empire collapsed, about four hundred years later, all that remained was the legend of a lost city. The wrath of Vesuvius had been forgotten.

Pompeii had vanished.

Eyewitness to Disaster

We actually have a firsthand account of what it was like to be in the area around Mount Vesuvius when the eruption occurred. In August A.D. 79, a seventeen-year-old boy named Pliny the Younger was visiting his uncle, Pliny the Elder, a famous admiral and author, at the naval base at Misenum. The town was located across the Bay of Naples from Pompeii. A few years after the disaster, the Roman historian Tacitus asked Pliny the Younger to write about what he had seen and experienced. The resulting detailed account was the first description ever of a volcanic eruption. It is a very vivid account. Pliny's writing captures the awesome nature of the disaster and the human suffering it brought:

A black and dreadful cloud bursting out in gusts of . . . serpentine [snakelike] vapor now and again yawned open to reveal long, fantastic flames, resembling flashes of lightning but much larger. Soon afterward, the cloud began to descend upon the earth and cover the sea. Ashes now fell upon us, though as yet in no great quantity. I looked behind me; darkness came rolling over the land after us like a torrent. I proposed, while we yet could see, to turn aside, lest we should be knocked down in the road by a crowd that followed us, and trampled to death in the dark. We had scarce sat down when darkness overspread us, not like that of a moonless or cloudy night, but of a room when it is shut up and the lamp put out. You could hear the shrieks of women and crying children and the shouts of men; some were seeking their children, others their parents; some praying to die, from the very fear of dying; many lifting their hands to the gods; but the greater part imagining that there were no gods left anywhere, that the last and eternal night was come upon the world.

A modern artist imagines the flight of the terrified people in Pompeii as they tried to escape the fallout from the sky.

2

REDISCOVERY

For more than 1,500 years, the buried city of Pompeii remained undisturbed. People looking for water stumbled upon the remains of Pompeii, but no one made the connection between a few ruins and a lost city. Then, in 1710, a well digger discovered the theater of Herculaneum. Soon people were digging up ancient treasures and carrying them off to decorate their homes or to sell. But the volcanic material that covered Herculaneum had hardened into a rocky layer that was up to sixty-five feet (20 meters) deep in places. Herculaneum was very difficult to excavate. Treasure hunters began looking for easier loot.

◄ *The remains of Pompeii see the light of day again after being excavated.*

In 1748 excavators began to dig at Pompeii. Off and on for more than a hundred years, Pompeii was explored and looted. At the time, southern Italy was undergoing constant political change. Some rulers supported the excavations at Pompeii and others did not. When Italy was finally united in 1860, the new ruler, King Victor Emmanuel II, became interested in properly investigating Pompeii. He put an archaeologist named Giuseppe Fiorelli in charge of excavations there.

Fiorelli was very organized about his work. He had the many piles of dirt that lay around Pompeii removed and the streets cleared so the plan of the city could be seen. Then he divided the city into nine regions. Within each region, he numbered the city blocks, called *insulae*, or "islands." Within each *insula*, he numbered each doorway so that every home and shop had its own label. For example, the house labeled 1.6.4. is house 4 in *insula* 6 of region l. It is the house of a man named Valerius Rufus and was in the process of being decorated when the disaster struck.

The Plan of the City

Before its destruction, Pompeii was a thriving city covering about 160 acres (64 hectares). Estimates of its population run from 6,400 to 30,000, but most experts think that between 8,000 and 12,000 people lived there year-round. Other people came during the hottest months to spend the summer by the sea.

Vesuvius's volcanic soil, full of minerals that help nourish plants, provided rich farmland outside the city. The most important crops were olives and grapes. Some of the olives were made into oil—oil presses have been found both in the city and in the remains of the farms that dotted Vesuvius's slopes. The region was famous for its sweet wine made from grapes grown in the abundant vineyards that thrived on the volcanic soil.

Pompeii's beautiful location, less than one-third of a mile (five hundred meters) from the Mediterranean Sea, and its mild, pleasant climate attracted craftspeople such as glassblowers and potters as well as fishers and traders. In addition to towns and villages, the shore of

Streets divide the city into blocks that resemble islands, which are called insulae.

Gladiators

Gladiatorial games were immensely popular in ancient Pompeii. They were so well liked that the amphitheater in Pompeii was big enough to hold the entire population of the city! While these bloody entertainments were favored by people in the Roman Empire, they originated with earlier tribes that had lived in Italy.

Gladiators were mostly slaves or criminals forced to fight, usually to the death, to provide excitement for an audience. There were many different kinds of gladiators. One kind fought with a short sword and carried a round shield, while another fought with a dagger, a fisherman's trident (three-pronged spear), and a net. Some rode horses; others had to fight blindfolded. In some events, a gladiator armed like a hunter had to chase and kill a wild animal such as a lion or an elephant.

Most gladiators lived very short lives. When one was badly wounded in a fight with another gladiator, a referee stopped the contest. The crowd yelled and cheered, trying to influence the organizer of the games either to show mercy or to tell the winner to finish the job and kill his wounded opponent. If the wounded man had fought well, his life might be spared. Otherwise, the victor delivered the deathblow. For good measure, an official clubbed the defeated gladiator to make sure he was thoroughly dead. Then the body was dragged by a hook through a narrow passage on the west side, called the Gate of Death.

A brave and expert gladiator

This wall painting from Pompeii shows a gladiator facing-off a lion. ➤

lucky enough to stay alive could become a popular idol. Such a gladiator was rarely killed, even if he lost a fight. He could become rich. If he managed to survive three years of combat, he was set free.

When the amphitheater and surrounding buildings at Pompeii were excavated, a great deal of the gladiators' equipment, such as helmets and ankle guards, was found. So were the skeletons of more than fifty of these unfortunate fighters. Two of them had died chained to a wall.

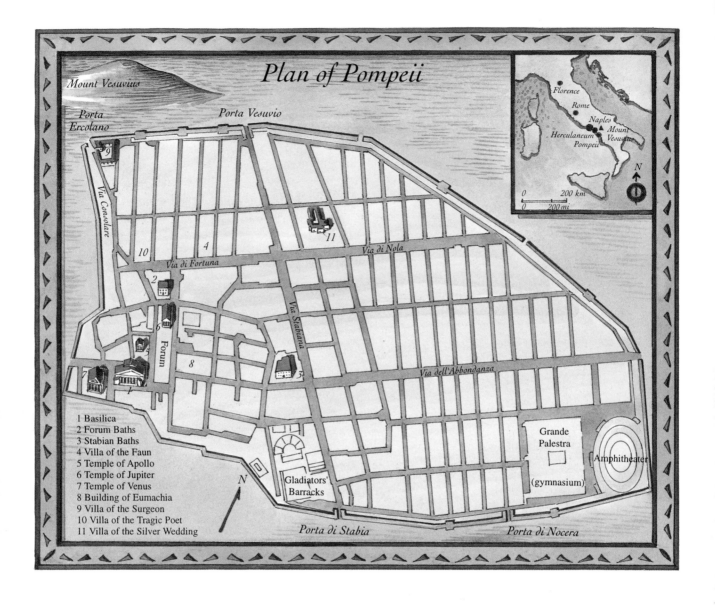

Plan of Pompeii

Mount Vesuvius

Porta Vesuvio

Porta Ercolano

Via Consolare

Via di Fortuna

Via di Nola

Via Stabiana

Via dell'Abbondanza

Forum

Porta di Stabia

Porta di Nocera

Grande Palestra
(gymnasium)

Amphitheater

Gladiators' Barracks

N

Florence
Rome
Naples
Herculaneum
Pompeii
Mount Vesuvius

N

0   200 km
0   200 mi

1 Basilica
2 Forum Baths
3 Stabian Baths
4 Villa of the Faun
5 Temple of Apollo
6 Temple of Jupiter
7 Temple of Venus
8 Building of Eumachia
9 Villa of the Surgeon
10 Villa of the Tragic Poet
11 Villa of the Silver Wedding

the Bay of Naples was dotted with large estates, called villas, used by rich Romans to escape the summer heat.

Leisure was important to the people of Pompeii. About 10 percent of the city was devoted to theaters, baths, and exercise areas. At the edge of town was an amphitheater, an oval open-air building much like a modern football stadium. The amphitheater was large enough to hold 20,000 people. The gladiatorial fights that so entertained the

Romans were held there. Another beautiful, horseshoe-shaped theater that seated 5,000 was built into a hillside. Plays and religious pageants were staged there, under a giant awning that protected spectators from the hot sun. A smaller theater for 1,500 people had a wooden roof and was the site of readings, speeches, and musical concerts. Three public baths offered relaxation and an opportunity for exercise.

The Forum, a plaza about 500 feet (152 meters) long and 150 feet (45 meters) wide, served as the legal and business center of the community. A wall at one end of the plaza was used for posting notices such as new laws and the outcome of trials. The notices were drawn on the white wall in black or red paint by special artists who could make beautiful letters. When the notices became outdated, they were

The Forum was once the center of activity in Pompeii.

covered with whitewash. During election campaigns, the wall held signs praising the virtues of the candidates, just like campaign posters do today.

People often gathered in the Forum to gossip and shop. A weekly Saturday market brought vendors from the countryside. They sold their produce from stalls erected under two-story rows of columns that lined the Forum on three sides. All sorts of foods were sold at the market—fruits and vegetables, grains, spices, and live fish, as well as prepared foods.

A temple honoring the powerful god Jupiter stood at the far end of the Forum. Just outside the columns of the marketplace were public buildings such as a law court and city offices. With its graceful columns, statues of famous people past and present, and brightly painted buildings, the Forum was an attractive place to pass the time.

Most of Pompeii consisted of homes and small businesses located in the *insulae*. There were bakeries, cloth-making shops, artisans' shops, and laundries. Gardens dotted the *insulae*. Almost 10 percent of the land in town was devoted to gardens that produced grapes, olives, fruits, and vegetables. Decorative gardens with flowers and bushes also abounded.

A wall with eight gates surrounded and protected the city. The main streets extended from a gate on one side, through the city, to a gate at the other side. The gates were closed at night and reopened each morning. When peace and prosperity came to the region in about 88 B.C., the walls at the southwest corner of the city, which faced the sea, were taken down. Large homes with beautiful sea views were built along the cliffs.

Providing for the Public

In some ways, Pompeii was like a modern city. But in others, it was very different from the cities we know today. Most of its streets were narrow, no more than fifteen feet (4.6 meters) wide. The widest were a little more than twenty-three feet (7 meters). Most streets were paved with lava rock from Vesuvius and lined with raised sidewalks and stone curbs. Some streets were used so much that the wheels of carts made ruts in the rock.

Like other Roman towns, Pompeii had a sewer system, but it was incomplete. The streets were raised in the center and sloped to gutters on the side. Sidewalks sloped toward the streets. This way all rainwater flowed through the gutters. However, drains to funnel water out of the streets were rare, and many of the roads must have remained wet after a rain. People probably also threw liquid wastes into the streets. At

Pompeii and the Roman Empire

The mighty Roman Empire ruled much of the Mediterranean region for centuries. At the beginning of the first century B.C., Pompeii was an ally of Rome but independent from it. Then, from 91 to 88 B.C., Rome battled its Italian allies, including Pompeii, and won. Around 88 B.C., Pompeii was named a *municipum*—a city in the provinces, dependent on Rome. Its citizens became Roman citizens. The city governed itself, but it had to remain loyal to Rome.

Rome's hold on Pompeii was strengthened in 80 B.C., when Latin became the official language and the Roman system of weights and measures became the standard. The laws of the city were changed to be more like Roman laws. Much of the land was taken away from local residents and given to five thousand Roman war veterans, greatly increasing Pompeii's Roman population.

In A.D. 79, many, perhaps most, of Pompeii's citizens were Romans, but some were from other cultures that had lived in the area for generations. Because it was a trading center, Pompeii was also home to people from around the Mediterranean, especially Greeks.

When the eruption of Mount Vesuvius destroyed Pompeii, the Roman Empire was in the middle of a two-hundred-year period of peace and prosperity. The Romans built roads that allowed people and goods to move easily from place to place. They encouraged trade and the development of industries such as cloth making, which was very important in Pompeii. Art, literature, and education were also valued. The Romans admired Greek civilization, which had come before them, and much of their art and writing was influenced by Greek culture.

corners, stepping-stones (with spaces between for cart wheels) allowed pedestrians to cross the streets without getting their feet wet or dirty.

For many years, the people of Pompeii got their water from the nearby Sarno River, from wells, and from rainwater collection. But then an aqueduct was built that brought water down from the surrounding hills. The water was carried to public baths, public fountains, and the homes of the wealthy by lead pipes under the sidewalks. People without their own water supply could get water from the public fountains. The three dozen or so fountains in Pompeii were almost all located on street corners, and most homes were no farther than eighty-five yards (78 meters) from a fountain, so the water didn't have to be carried far.

◄ *Pompeii's streets were so busy that chariot wheels dug ruts in them. Here you can see the ruts running up the street past the stepping-stones. People walked on the stones to keep their feet dry when crossing the street.*

3

LIVING IN POMPEII

People in Pompeii lived in a society where everyone was ranked by wealth and social standing. Some people were citizens; others were slaves or free men and women. Some people were rich. Many were poor. A few were middle-class. While wealthy citizens pursued politics and pleasure, craftspeople and shopkeepers worked hard to make a living.

The Value of Citizenship
Every person born in the United States is automatically a citizen. People who come from other countries can also become citizens. All the people living in the United States must

Beautiful frescoes, or wall paintings, decorated homes in Pompeii. This picture is a modern artist's idea of the way the house of one wealthy family may have looked. ➤

obey the same laws, and all have the same protection under the laws, whether they are citizens or not.

Things were different in the Roman Empire. Citizenship was a special privilege that made life much easier. A person became a citizen if he was born of citizen parents, if he completed military service, or if citizenship was granted by the authorities. Even though anyone could get married, only the marriages of citizens were legal. Married citizens could legally pass on their property to their children. Noncitizens had no such assurance. The business dealings of citizens were regulated by consistent laws. This was especially important to traders, who often bought and sold goods in different parts of the empire. If they were citizens, they were always subject to the same rules and laws. Only adult citizens with a certain amount of property could serve as town councillors, a position of honor and power.

Slaves in Roman Times

Slaves were common in the Roman Empire. Approximately one-third of the people living in Pompeii may have been slaves. Slaves might be soldiers or the descendants of soldiers who had been captured in war. They might be men and women purchased by the Romans in foreign slave markets. Many unfortunate people were enslaved after being captured at sea by pirates. Slaves could be Greek, Macedonian, Turkish, Syrian, Jewish, Sicilian, or African, for example. They were considered property. They could be bought and sold, and they could be inherited as well. They had little or no legal rights. Life could be very hard for slaves who worked in mines or who were forced to fight in the amphitheater as entertainment for an audience.

Even poor freeborn families might have two or three slaves to do work such as cooking or housekeeping. Rich people might have hundreds of slaves, including professionals such as doctors and teachers for their children. Family slaves were often educated and skilled and

The man in this wall painting was probably an educated slave who tutored the child. ➤

might be treated well. They were respected for their talents, and their children might play with those of the family. Slave owners sometimes freed a slave. The slave would then take on his former master's family name and might continue to work in the household.

Homes in Pompeii

The eruption of Mount Vesuvius caught the people of Pompeii in the midst of their daily lives. At most archaeological sites, only some everyday objects are found. These are often worn-out things that people had thrown away. But at Pompeii, Herculaneum, and other sites near Vesuvius, human life stopped abruptly in A.D. 79. Objects were preserved together as sets—pots and pans in a kitchen, or combs and mirrors in a bedroom.

Archaeological sites are usually made up of buildings that people have abandoned for one reason or another. But in Pompeii, many buildings were preserved in perfect condition, complete with the furniture and wall decorations.

This finely made case was found in Pompeii with its original contents—makeup items—still intact.

The atrium *of a typical upper-class family's house had a basin in the floor for catching rainwater.*

The excavations reveal much about how the typical upper-class family lived in Roman times. The one- or two-story home of a wealthy family had many rooms, including a kitchen, dining room, and bedrooms. People entered the home through a wide entrance with double doors. The entrance led into a covered courtyard called the *atrium*, where guests were received. The *atrium* was decorated with wall paintings and beautiful furniture. Before the aqueduct was built, households used rainwater collected through spouts leading from the *atrium* roof to a basin in the floor.

A dinner in Pompeii. Meals were times for people to relax and enjoy one another's company.

Meals in Pompeii

E ven in the first century A.D., people were sometimes in a hurry and caught a meal on the run from a fast-food restaurant. In Pompeii snack bars had a counter with holes that held pottery vessels containing warm food and drinks. The menu was limited—meat, goat cheese, lentil or bean stew, and warm wine.

At home, people enjoyed dining. Instead of sitting down to eat, people in Roman times ate lying on their left sides. They supported themselves on their left arms and ate with their right hands. The dining table had sloping couches on three sides. Each couch had room for three diners. The floor of the dining room might be beautifully decorated with a mosaic, a picture made by fitting together bits of stone, glass, or tiles of different colors. The picture might show abundant sea life, creatures that could end up as food on the table. Wall paintings might feature luscious fruits or beautiful vegetables to encourage the diners' appetites.

People often invited guests over for dinner. At the dining table, the master of the house lay at the inside place on the couch to the left of the table. His wife was next to him, with his son or a favored freed slave next to her. The guest of honor reclined on the inner couch, closest to the host.

Slaves cut up the meat before it was served, and the diners ate with their fingers or a spoon. The first course was often a selection of small items such as olives and cooked eggs, similar to what Italians today call antipasto. The main dish was often fish, for the Bay of Naples provided a generous harvest of delicious seafood. Game birds, lamb, and pork were also popular. The people enjoyed pungent spices such as black pepper, cumin, and bay leaves. Fruits like figs and plums were often cooked with the meat. Sauces such as a sweet-and-sour sauce or a very salty sauce made from fermented fish often accompanied the meal.

Dessert consisted of fresh fruits such as cherries or grapes, along with cakes or other sweets. A favorite dessert was honeyed eggs—eggs beaten with olive oil and cooked, then served with honey and pepper on top.

Lunch had been served in many houses just before Vesuvius erupted at 1:00 P.M. The food was left on the tables as the people struggled to survive the disaster. The flow that engulfed Herculaneum preserved the food better than the ash and rock that at first covered Pompeii. In one house in Herculaneum, a meal of eggs, bread, salad, fruit, and cake still remained on the table.

At the far end of the *atrium* was a large room called the *tablinum*. In Pompeii's earlier days, the *tablinum* was used as the master bedroom. But over time, it became a place for storing family documents, which were written on waxed wooden tablets, and for visiting with guests. Wooden screens or curtains covered the opening from the *atrium* into the *tablinum*.

The kitchen was a relatively simple room, usually located off to one side of the *atrium*. It had an oven, a hearth, and a sink. Pots and pans made from bronze or pottery hung on the walls. Food was cooked in pots with short legs, which stood over smoldering charcoal on the hearth. Some food was baked in the wood-fired oven.

Each home had a small room just big enough for the toilet. This room was near the kitchen, where the water used to flush away wastes was kept. The toilet could also be used for pouring away kitchen wastewater. Some toilets appear to have been connected to a sewer system, while others led to a pit in the ground.

Even though the homes in Pompeii were crowded into the blocks known as *insulae*, each homeowner found room for a small garden. Like home gardens today, some featured decorative trees and bushes while others had fruit trees, grapevines, and herb and vegetable plants. The walls surrounding the gardens were painted with realistic scenes of plants and flowers or of wild animals, such as lions chasing their prey. The walls of a small garden might be painted to look like additional garden space, with a fountain, roses in bloom, and wild birds. The paintings blended into the real garden, making it look larger than it was. Large homes often had a garden called a peristyle. It was surrounded by graceful columns and might contain fountains and an outdoor dining room.

Bedrooms in Pompeii tended to be small and windowless. The Roman love of nature was expressed in these rooms by wall paintings of birds and flowers, which re-created the outdoors. Beds had a metal frame that held wooden supports for the mattress. The bedroom served as a dressing room, too. Both Pompeii and Herculaneum have yielded many combs, hairpins, mirrors, and cosmetic jars, as well as

Many homes in Pompeii had beautiful peristyle gardens.

Realistic paintings of birds and flowers brought nature closer to city dwellers.

beautiful jewelry. In addition to rings, necklaces, and bracelets, Roman women wore decorative armbands, often in the form of a snake. Roman boys who were born free wore a special neckpiece called a bulla to show their status.

Working-class people in Pompeii didn't live in spacious homes. Servants lived in apartments or rooms on the second floor of the house where they worked. The poor often lived in small rooms built into the fronts of the houses. Stairs from the street led up to balconies in front of the rooms. A large block of apartments by the waterfront also housed many families.

Making Things

In Roman times, products were made in small shops, not big factories. Pompeii was a center for making cloth goods. Most clothing was made from wool, which came from sheep that grazed in nearby fields. Archaeologists have been able to identify workshops where felt was made, cloth was dyed, linen (made from the flax plant) was woven, and so forth. One of the largest buildings around the Forum was the headquarters for the clothworkers. It was called the Building of Eumachia. It probably served as the clothworkers, meeting place. Both raw wool and woven cloth were also stored and displayed there.

People in any town need tools and other metal products. Shops specializing in making items from bronze and from iron have been found in Pompeii. Bronze scales were used to weigh the goods people bought. The many sets of scales found in Pompeii are just like the ones used by shopkeepers in Naples today.

Shops lined the Forum and the main east-west street of the town, which archaeologists have named the Via dell'Abbondanza (street of abundance). The street sides of many buildings also held small stores. Many houses in Pompeii had been converted into businesses, perhaps after being damaged in the earthquake of A.D. 62. Shop owners might conveniently live above their workplaces. Slaves often did the manual work, while the owners managed the business.

The remains of a bakery on the outskirts of the city. You can see the millstone, once powered by a donkey, in front of the large oven.

Baking Bread

Bread has been an important part of the European diet for thousands of years. Because of the excavations at Pompeii, we know a lot more about how bread was made in Roman times.

Making bread began with milling the flour. Twenty of Pompeii's thirty or more bakeries had their own mills. The bakeries with mills lay in the outer parts of the city, especially to the north. The grainfields were in that direction, so grain could be delivered easily, avoiding the crowded downtown streets. Bakeries without mills were concentrated in the center of the city.

Grain mills in Pompeii were usually operated with the help of a donkey. The animal would walk around and around the millstone, turning it so that it crushed and ground the grain. In some mills, slaves instead of donkeys turned the stone.

Once the grain was ground, it could be made into dough. Usually, the dough was shaped into round loaves. Each loaf was scored with lines so that the bread could be broken into pie-shaped wedges. For special occasions, the dough might be placed in molds of different fancy shapes.

After rising, the loaves were baked in wood-fired ovens. The bread ovens of Pompeii looked very much like the pizza ovens of present-day Naples. They had an arched opening and a flat stone floor. The fire was built on the oven floor. When the oven was hot enough, the ashes were raked out and the bread was put in to bake.

Some bakeries in Pompeii were quite large. One had four mills and a huge oven. It contained eighty-one loaves that had been baking when Vesuvius came to life.

Many loaves of bread like this one were found in the ruins.

4

A DAY IN POMPEII

Many writings describing life in Roman times survive to this day. By combining these written records with the findings at Pompeii and other sites, archaeologists can get a good idea of how people lived nearly two thousand years ago. Most of the writings are about wealthy, influential people. Such people also left more of their possessions behind, so we know more about them than we do about slaves or the poor.

Telling Time

Romans didn't measure time the way we do. For us, every day has 24 hours, each of equal length throughout the year. The Romans also had a 24-hour day. But they wanted each day to have exactly

◄ *This wall painting of a baker's shop was found among the ruins of Pompeii. From it we can get a glimpse of everyday life in the city.*

12 hours of daylight and 12 hours of night. So they adjusted the length of an hour, making it longer or shorter, depending on the season. In Rome the shortest winter day has 540 minutes of daylight. On that day, the Romans made each hour shorter—just 45 minutes long. The longest summer day in Rome has 900 minutes of daylight. So on that day, each Roman hour was stretched to 75 minutes.

For this reason, when we talk about a day in Roman Pompeii, we say that activities occurred during the sixth hour, the eighth hour, the eleventh hour, and so forth. The halfway point in the day was the beginning of the seventh hour. This always came at the same moment in real time, no matter the season. Many activities began at the seventh hour, after an hour of rest.

Patrons and *Clientes*

A day in Pompeii began at dawn. Farmers went to their fields. Shopkeepers began setting up for the day. Children hurried to school. And *clientes* appeared in front of the houses of their patrons.

The wealthy in Roman times held all the power and authority. But they also had a responsibility to the ordinary people. Each wealthy man, called a patron, had a group of followers called *clientes*. The relationship between *clientes* and patrons was very important. It was even passed on through the generations, so that the son of a patron inherited his father's *clientes* and their descendants as his own *clientes*. The patron provided some financial aid to his *clientes*, while they gave him political support. Some *clientes* were former slaves who had been freed by their patron. Others were poor freemen. Still other *clientes* were more like beggars, going from one patron to another in search of handouts.

The homes of the patrons often had a protected area in front of the doors where the *clientes* could wait, sheltered from the elements. At dawn the doors opened, and the *clientes* gathered in the *atrium*. One by one, they entered the *tablinum* to meet with their patron. By the end of the second hour, the meetings had finished.

The patron then left for the Forum, often accompanied by some

Many houses in Pompeii and Herculaneum had protected areas built onto their fronts. This street was uncovered in Herculaneum.

of his *clientes*. The Forum was a center for business, finance, politics, and government. Law courts in the Forum opened at the beginning of the third hour and might stay in session until the end of the ninth hour. If his patron was involved in court, a *cliente* was expected to be present.

Religion in Pompeii

The Romans had so many gods that, according to one author, in some towns there were more gods than people. Each god had his or her own personality and sphere of influence. Each was believed to be immortal but had human virtues and failings.

The most powerful Roman deity was Jupiter, the king of the gods and guardian of the Roman state. Venus, the goddess of love, was regarded as an ancestor of the Romans. She watched over gardens and cultivated fields. A large temple in Pompeii was dedicated to Venus, and her image appeared all over the city, on everything from the walls of gladiators' rooms to shop and tavern signs. Apollo, an important God who had come to Italy from Greece, shared the guardianship of Pompeii with Venus. While many temples were not repaired after the earthquake of A.D. 62, Apollo's was fully restored.

The mythical hero Hercules was the oldest guardian of Pompeii. He was said to have founded the city. Hercules was the son of Jupiter and a human mother. Though he wasn't strictly a god, he was sometimes worshipped like one. Hercules was famous for traveling far and wide to perform a number of difficult tasks, called the labors of Hercules. Because he was thought to offer protection on long journeys, he was especially popular in Pompeii, where so many merchants and traders lived. The image of Hercules appeared in numerous paintings in Pompeii, and statues of him abounded there as well.

Each Roman household in Pompeii also had its own guardian spirits, called the lares and penates. Every home had a shrine dedicated to the lares and penates, and the family made offerings of food and wine to them at every meal. Small statues of these spirits were found in many homes in Pompeii. Honored along with the lares and penates were the spirits of the family's ancestors.

Some people were not satisfied with many of the formal rituals and traditions of the Roman religion. They wanted a personal god to help guide them through life. Such people turned to "mystery religions." These were religions centering around ceremonies that celebrated the death and rebirth of a god. In the festival of the Roman goddess Ceres, people remembered the yearly return of Ceres' daughter Persephone from the underworld kingdom of Pluto. In the feast honoring Bacchus, Roman god of wine, worshippers dined, danced, and drank themselves into a state of unearthly ecstasy.

Religions brought from other parts of the world, especially the Middle East, were also practiced in Pompeii. In the myth of Cybele, a goddess from the region that is now Turkey, people celebrated the rebirth of her dead lover Attis.

The most popular deity that was not Roman or Greek was the mother goddess of the Egyptian religion, Isis. Her temple was only a short distance from the Forum. Worship of Isis had been brought to Pompeii by slaves, traders, and sailors. Like the temple of Apollo, the temple of Isis was quickly rebuilt after the A.D. 62 earthquake.

Isis was revered as a good mother, a faithful wife, the Queen of Heaven, the Queen of War, the Lawgiver, and the Glory of Women. Like worshippers in other mystery religions, her followers were promised a personal resurrection, or life after death.

Small statues once stood in this household altar dedicated to the family's guardian spirits.

Some patrons held political office. Two *duumvirs*, or mayors, supervised the meetings of the legislature and other political activities. Another two officials were in charge of maintaining public services such as the streets and water supplies. They also gave out licenses for new businesses. The city had a town council, which was very large by modern standards: eighty to a hundred members, who served for life.

While the wealthy and their *clientes* concerned themselves with politics and business, most of the other people of Pompeii were hard at work. Bakeries had opened before dawn, and shops had also opened early, usually by the second hour. They might close and reopen during the day, depending on other activities such as rest time or visits by the wealthy to the baths.

When a wealthy man was not involved in extra public business such as a long court session, his working day ended at the sixth hour. At this time, the baths were at their hottest, and the upper classes headed there to exercise and bathe. This pleasant part of the day could last as long as three hours. Most people, however, probably had to wait until the tenth hour or later, when their work was done, to bathe.

Public Baths

The Roman people believed in cleanliness. Homes of some of the wealthier Romans had their own baths, but most people went to the public baths. These were large establishments something like modern health clubs, where people could play games, exercise, get a massage, swim, and bathe.

The Stabian baths were the largest of Pompeii's three public baths. They had been badly damaged by the A.D. 62 earthquake, but the women's area was still being used in A.D. 79. The men's area at the Stabian baths was much larger than the women's. The women had only a few rooms: a changing room, a cold bath, a warm room, and a hot room. The men had these plus a large swimming pool and an outdoor exercise area.

The heating system at the baths was quite effective. In the hot and warm rooms, there were hollow spaces between the walls and

A mosaic of sea creatures decorates the floor of the women's baths in Herculaneum. The Romans loved to decorate with mosaics.

under the floor to allow heat to circulate. Hot air from the central furnace was channeled to holes under the raised floors of the hot rooms. After heating the hot rooms, the now-cooler air passed on to heat the warm rooms.

When people came to bathe, they first removed their clothes in the changing room. In the warm room, slaves rubbed the bathers' bodies with ointment. The Romans believed it was important to move gradually from cold to hot and back again, so the warm room was kept at a constant moderately warm temperature. After warming up, the bathers put on wooden sandals to protect their feet from the hot floor and went into the hot room. There they would relax and sweat. Next,

In this modern painting, the artist imagines how an upper-class woman in Pompeii might have relaxed in her home.

they would take a hot bath, either in an individual tub or in the heated pool, which held about eight people.

A cold bath followed, then a return to the hot room to sweat once more. After this, a slave used a special tool called a strigil to scrape the bather's body. A cold dip was the last step in the bathing sequence.

Women and Children

We know less about the daily activities of wealthy women than we do about their husbands. While wealthy men held the power, their wives probably spent much of their time supervising the slaves and making sure that the household ran smoothly.

Education was important for the children of the upper class. Boys usually had their own tutors, who might be educated slaves, or they went to school, where they learned in small classes. Girls were usually taught domestic skills, such as spinning, weaving, and sewing, at home by their mothers. Some girls might have a tutor or attend elementary school for a time. Slaves who had some education often accompanied the children to school, so they would know what lessons their charges had to learn.

Upper-class children in Pompeii had pets and toys. Paintings often show children with dogs and birds, although cats and rabbits also served as pets. For toys they had dolls with miniature furniture and pots and pans, bronze and pottery animals, rattles, and games. Some lucky children got to ride in carts drawn by goats, while others entertained themselves on seesaws and swings. They played games children still know today, such as hide-and-seek. Marbles and dice have been found in Pompeii, along with hoops and tops.

Poor children weren't so fortunate. One wall painting in Pompeii shows children working hard, cleaning cloth by trampling it in vats. The job must have been unpleasant, for cloth was stiffened with human urine before being put into the vats with cleansing agents.

5

STUDYING POMPEII

Pompeii is an unusual archaeological treasure for many reasons. It is a place caught in time, frozen by disaster in the middle of a typical day. But was the eruption of Mount Vesuvius the only event that stopped the city in its tracks? Or were previous disasters, mainly the earthquake of A.D. 62 and perhaps others that followed, the real cause of its doom?

These unfortunate people died in their home. ➤

Archaeologists argue these questions today. Some believe that Pompeii was crippled by the quake and that many people left the city, abandoning their homes. Others see signs that when Vesuvius erupted, the city was rising from the quake's rubble and being restored to beauty.

Fiorelli's Gift

Without the work of Giuseppe Fiorelli from 1860 to 1875, Pompeii could easily have been lost to science through further looting and destruction. Fiorelli did more than develop an efficient way of labeling buildings in the city. His larger goal was to completely uncover and reveal the secrets of a vanished culture. He worked in thorough fashion, completing the study of one area before moving on to the next. Before his time, some objects such as furniture and even wall paintings had been removed and displayed in museums. Fiorelli left finds in their rightful place whenever possible so that they could help show how people had lived in A.D. 79. He kept detailed records of his excavations so that others would know what work had already been done and exactly where things had been found.

Fiorelli helped bring Pompeii back to life with his scientific work and careful attention to detail. But perhaps his greatest gift to the imagination was his method of recovering the human agony of the disaster. He knew that when the ash and rock fell, they settled on everything, cloaking every object. This included the victims of the eruption. He also knew that rain after the eruption had soaked the ash, which hardened when it dried. Inside their ashen cocoons, the bodies of the dead would have rotted away, leaving hollows where once there had been flesh.

Fiorelli decided to try to recover the moment of death by pouring liquid plaster of Paris into cavities that workmen came across in their excavations. The plaster filled the cavities and hardened, reproducing the shapes captured by the ash. When the plaster was removed, it revealed moments of terror and agony—a woman holding a baby, with two of her children hanging onto her clothing; a dog wearing a spiked collar, still tied to a post in a yard; a man with his arm thrown

A victim of Mount Vesuvius's rage, caught frozen in time

protectively over the face of a pregnant woman. Using Fiorelli's method, casts of dozens of bodies workers have made through the years of excavation at Pompeii. The technique has also been used to preserve the shapes of other objects, such as wooden doors that had deteriorated over time.

Discoveries Today and Tomorrow

In the early days after its discovery, Pompeii's beautiful paintings, mosaics, and other art were the focus of much study. Now researchers are more interested in who lived in Pompeii and how they lived. Were

In this wall painting from Pompeii, a musician plays a kithara, an ancient stringed instrument. Researchers continue to study the lost city of Pompeii in hopes of learning more about the way people lived long ago.

most of the people Romans or were they native inhabitants of the region? What were the relationships between the rich and the poor? What more can we learn about daily life?

Another focus of recent work is Pompeii before A.D. 79. The city was inhabited for hundreds of years before the fateful eruption that ended its living history. Archaeologists are now carefully digging deeper in the site to find out about the city's earlier inhabitants.

Although Pompeii has been studied for more than a hundred years, this unique site still holds many secrets waiting to be revealed. Archaeologists will be exploring the ruins and sifting the evidence for years to come. And we will continue to be fascinated by the once beautiful and lively city that, in one terrifying moment, was frozen in time.

Pompeii in Time

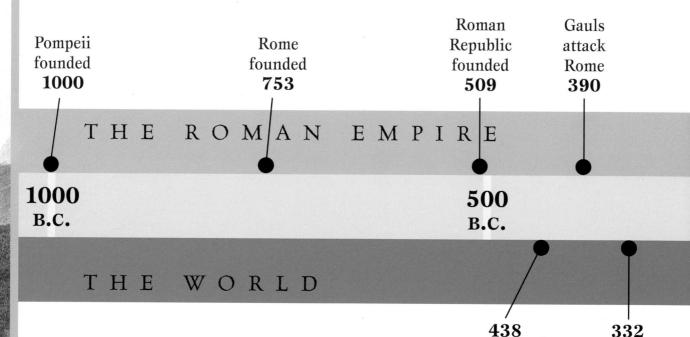

| Pompeii founded **1000** | Rome founded **753** | Roman Republic founded **509** | Gauls attack Rome **390** |

THE ROMAN EMPIRE

1000
B.C.

500
B.C.

THE WORLD

438
Parthenon
completed
in Athens,
Greece

332
Alexander
the Great
conquers
Persia

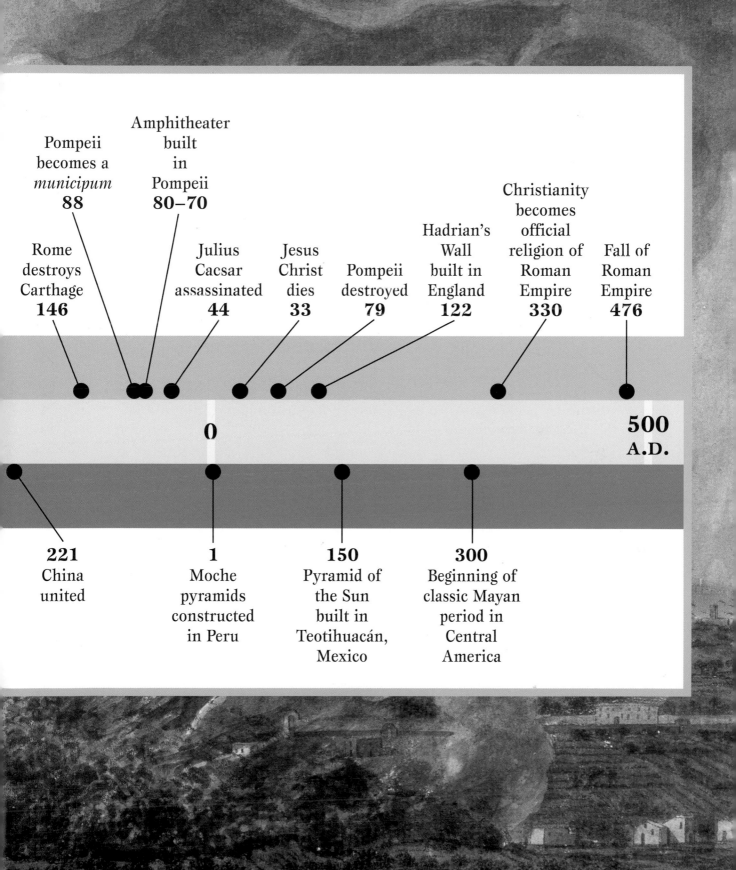

Pompeii
becomes a
municipum
88

Amphitheater
built
in
Pompeii
80–70

Rome
destroys
Carthage
146

Julius
Cacsar
assassinated
44

Jesus
Christ
dies
33

Pompeii
destroyed
79

Hadrian's
Wall
built in
England
122

Christianity
becomes
official
religion of
Roman
Empire
330

Fall of
Roman
Empire
476

0

**500
A.D.**

221
China
united

1
Moche
pyramids
constructed
in Peru

150
Pyramid of
the Sun
built in
Teotihuacán,
Mexico

300
Beginning of
classic Mayan
period in
Central
America

Glossary

amphitheater: An oval arena used in ancient Rome. Rows of seats surrounded an open space in the center where performances took place, much like our modern football stadiums.

aqueduct: A large pipe or other channel that carries water from one place to another, using the force of gravity.

archaeologist: A scientist who studies pottery, tools, weapons, and other remains of ancient cultures to see how people lived.

artisan: A person who is skilled in a particular craft.

atrium: The inner courtyard of a Roman house.

avalanche: The swift, sudden fall of a mass of material down a mountain slope.

bulla: A neckpiece worn by a freeborn boy in Roman times until he reached manhood.

clientes: Ordinary people who gave their patron political support in return for help such as financial aid.

core (of the earth): The liquid center of the planet, believed to consist of nickel and iron.

crust (of the earth): The solid outer layer of the planet.

debris: The bits and pieces of something that has been broken.

excavate: To uncover by digging.

gladiator: A man, usually a slave or criminal, forced to fight in an arena to entertain an audience.

insula (plural: *insulae*): An area like a city block, bordered on all sides by streets.

lava: Hot melted rock that comes out of an erupting volcano or through cracks in the earth's surface.

magma: Liquid rock material found under the earth's crust.

mantle: The layer of liquid rock between the earth's crust and the core.

mosaic: A picture or design made by arranging colored pieces of stone, tile, or glass and cementing them together.

municipum: A city in the provinces, which was dependent on Rome.

patron: A wealthy Roman citizen with *clientes*.

peristyle: A garden surrounded by columns.

pumice: A lightweight volcanic rock filled with tiny air bubbles.

site: The place where something is located or where something was found.

strigil: A tool used to clean a bather's body by scraping it.

tablinum: A large room at the far end of the *atrium,* used to receive visitors.

tectonic plates: The pieces of the earth's crust that float about on top of the mantle.

For Further Reading

Books

Biel, Timothy Levi. *Pompeii*. World Disasters Series. San Diego: Lucent Books, 1989.

Bisel, Sara C., Jane Bisel, and Shelley Tanaka. *The Secrets of Vesuvius*. New York: Scholastic, 1990.

Connolly, Peter. *Pompeii*. Oxford: Oxford University Press, 1990.

Corbishley, Mike. *The Roman World*. New York: Warwick Press, 1986.

Gore, Rick. "After 2,000 Years of Silence the Dead Do Tell Tales at Vesuvius." *National Geographic*, May 1984, pp. 557–613.

Judge, Joseph. "A Buried Roman Town Gives Up Its Dead." *National Geographic*, December 1982, pp. 687–693.

Maiuri, Amedeo. "Last Moments of the Pompeians." *National Geographic*, November 1961, pp. 651–669.

Reid, T. R. "The Power and the Glory of the Roman Empire." *National Geographic*, July 1997, pp. 2–41.

Websites*

http://www.volcano.und.nodak.edu/vwdocs/volc_images/imgund vesuvius.html

This website has pictures and information on Mount Vesuvius and other volcanoes.

http://www.harpy.uccs.edu/roman/html/pompeiislides.html

As well as showing images of the architecture in the city of Pompeii, this site has good links to other related information.

*Websites change from time to time. For additional on-line information, check with the media specialist at your local library.

Bibliography

Bon, Sara E., and Rick Jones. *Sequence and Space in Pompeii*. Oxbow Monograph 77. Oxford, England: Oxbow Books, 1997.

Connolly, Peter. *Pompeii*. Oxford: Oxford University Press, 1990.

Editors of Time-Life Books. *Pompeii: The Vanished City*. Alexandria, VA: Time-Life Books, 1992.

Fisher, Richard V., Grant Heiken, and Jeffrey B. Hulen. *Volcanoes: Crucibles of Change*. Princeton, NJ: Princeton University Press, 1997.

Laurence, Ray. *Roman Pompeii: Space and Society*. London: Routledge, 1994.

Leach, Maria, ed. *Funk & Wagnalls Standard Dictionary of Folklore, Mythology, and Legend*. New York: Harper & Row, 1984.

Levey, Judith S., and Agnes Greenhall, eds. *The Concise Columbia Encyclopedia*. New York: Columbia University Press, 1983.

Liversidge, Joan. *Everyday Life in the Roman Empire*. New York: G. P. Putnam's Sons, 1976.

Parslow, Christopher Charles. *Rediscovering Antiquity: Karl Weber and the Excavation of Herculaneum, Pompeii, and Stabiae*. New York: Cambridge University Press, 1995.

Scarre, Chris, ed. *Smithsonian Timelines of the Ancient World: A Visual Chronology from the Origins of Time to A.D. 1500*. New York: Dorling Kindersley, 1993.

Slayman, Andrew L. "The *New* Pompeii." *Archaeology*, November/December 1997, pp. 26–33.

Tanzer, Helen H. *The Common People of Pompeii: A Study of the Graffiti*. Baltimore: Johns Hopkins Press, 1939.

Wallace-Hadrill, Andrew. *Houses and Society in Pompeii and Herculaneum*. Princeton, NJ: Princeton University Press, 1994.

Index

Page numbers for illustrations are in **boldface**

About the Author

Dorothy Patent is the author of more than one hundred science and nature books for children and has won numerous awards for her writing. She has a Ph.D. in zoology from the University of California, Berkeley.

Although trained as a biologist, Dorothy has always been fascinated by the human past. At home, next to the books about animals, her shelves are jammed with titles such as *Mysteries of the Past.* When the opportunity came to write about other times and cultures for children, Dorothy plunged enthusiastically into the project. In the process of researching the FROZEN IN TIME series, she said, "I have had some great adventures and have come to understand much more deeply what it means to be human."

Dorothy lives in Missoula, Montana, with her husband, Greg, and their two dogs, Elsa and Ninja. They enjoy living close to nature in their home at the edge of a forest.